STECK-VAUGHN

PORTRAIT OF AMERICA

Delaware

Steck-Vaughn Company
Executive Editor	Diane Sharpe
Senior Editor	Martin S. Saiewitz
Design Manager	Pamela Heaney
Photo Editor	Margie Foster

Proof Positive/Farrowlyne Associates, Inc.
Program Editorial, Revision Development, Design, and Production

Consultants: Donald Porter, Delaware Tourism Office; Gigi Windley, Director, Delaware Tourism Office; James A. Stewart, Administrator, Delaware State Museums

Published by Raintree Steck-Vaughn Publishers, an imprint of Steck-Vaughn Company.

A Turner Educational Services, Inc. book. Based on the Portrait of America television series by R. E. (Ted) Turner.

Cover Photo: Cover photography of Delaware's capitol by © Holt Comfer / Grant Heilman Photography.

Library of Congress Cataloging-in-Publication Data

Thompson, Kathleen.
    Delaware / Kathleen Thompson.
        p. cm. — (Portrait of America)
    "Based on the Portrait of America television series"—T.p. verso.
    "A Turner book."
    Includes index.
    ISBN 0-8114-7328-7 (library binding).—ISBN 0-8114-7433-X (softcover)
    1. Delaware—Juvenile literature. [1. Delaware.] I. Portrait of America
(Television program) II. Title. III. Series: Thompson, Kathleen.
Portrait of America.
F164.3.T48 1996
975.1—dc20
                                    95-38249
                                        CIP
                                        AC

Printed and Bound in the United States of America

2 3 4 5 6 7 8 9 10 WZ 01 00 99 98

Acknowledgments
The publishers wish to thank the following for permission to reproduce photographs:
P. 7 Hagley Museum and Library; p. 8 Holy Trinity (Old Swedes) Church Foundation, Inc.; p. 10 © Frank Cezus/Tony Stone Images; p. 11 Delaware State Museum; p. 12 Historical Society of Delaware; p. 14 Delaware Tourism Office; p. 16 © Photri; p. 17 Delaware River and Bay Authority; p. 18 Historical Society of Pennsylvania; p. 19 Delaware State Museum; p. 20 Delaware State Travel Service; p. 22 Du Pont, Inc.; p. 23 (both) Delaware Department of Agriculture; p. 24 (both) Du Pont, Inc.; p. 25 Chrysler Corporation; p. 26 (top) © Marian Pohlman/Bombay Hook National Wildlife Refuge, (bottom) Delaware Tourism Office; p. 27 (both) Delaware Tourism Office; pp. 28, 29 Hagley Museum and Library; p. 30 Courtesy, Winterthur Museum; p. 31 (top) Richards, Layton & Finger, (bottom) Du Pont, Inc.; p. 32 Arden Media Resources; p. 33 (left) UPI/Bettmann, (right) Arden Media Resources; p. 34 © James Little/Brandywine Creek State Park; p. 36 (top) Delaware Tourism Office, (bottom) © Tony Boyd-Heron/Main Street Committee of Milton, Inc.; p. 37 Delaware Tourism Office; p. 38 (top) Courtesy, Winterthur Museum, (bottom) Nemours Mansion and Gardens; p. 39 Delaware Tourism Office; pp. 40, 41 (both) Courtesy, Delaware Folklife Program/Division of Parks and Recreation; p. 42 © Uniphoto; p. 44 Delaware Tourism Office; p. 46 One Mile Up; p. 47 (left) One Mile Up, (center, right) Delaware Tourism Office.

STECK-VAUGHN
PORTRAIT OF AMERICA

Delaware

Kathleen Thompson

A Turner Book

RAINTREE
STECK-VAUGHN
PUBLISHERS
The Steck-Vaughn Company

Austin, Texas

Delaware

Centerville
Wilmington
Newark
Newport
Christiana
New Castle
Delaware City
Chesapeake and
Delaware Canal
Odessa
Delaware River
Smyrna
BOMBAY HOOK NATIONAL
WILDLIFE REFUGE
DOVER
Mispillion River
Milford
Milton
Lewes
Rehoboth Beach
Seaford
Rehoboth
Bay
Laurel
Milsboro

Contents

Introduction

Small but mighty—that's Delaware. It's the second smallest state in terms of landmass. But during its long history, it's done big things. In fact, Delaware was the very first state to approve the United States Constitution back in 1787. That won Delaware the nickname "First State."

The people of Delaware think ahead. They have protected their historic sites and natural resources. Despite its small size, Delaware boasts 12 state parks. Whether you enjoy hiking, kite flying, sailing, or horse races, Delaware has something to offer. Proud of its reputation as the "First State," Delaware stays in charge of its own future.

The water wheel at the old Du Pont Powder Mill still operates. The Du Pont Powder Mill was built in the early 1800s to produce gunpowder.

Delaware

mill towns, broiler chickens, folklife traditions

The First State

On a stormy day in 1610, Samuel Argall, an English explorer from the colony of Virginia, needed shelter from the fierce Atlantic. He sailed into a bay about midway down the east coast of the North American continent. Thinking he had found something new, Argall gave the bay a name. He called it De La Warr Bay, after the governor of Virginia, Lord De La Warr.

Argall was not the first European explorer to discover the area we now call Delaware. Henry Hudson had explored the area for the Dutch the year before. The land was inhabited by two Native American groups, the Lenni-Lenape in the north, and the Nanticoke in the south.

The Nanticoke were a peaceful people who lived mainly by fishing and trapping. Their name means "tidewater people." The Lenni-Lenape were an Algonquian-speaking confederacy of three Native American groups: Munsee, Unalachtigo, and Unami. The English settlers called them the Delaware. The

Old Swedes Church, in Wilmington, is one of the oldest churches in the United States. Religious services have been held there regularly since 1698.

Lewes is the site of Delaware's oldest European settlement. Today, Lewes is mainly a fishing village and resort town.

Lenni-Lenape were mainly farmers who fished and hunted only to supplement their diet. Their name means "genuine people."

In 1631 the Dutch founded a small settlement near the present-day town of Lewes. They named it *Zwaanendael*, which means "valley of the swans." The settlement was destroyed due to a misunderstanding between coastal Native Americans and the Dutch.

Seven years later Swedish colonists settled along the Christina River and called their colony New Sweden. They then built Fort Christina, which became present-day Wilmington.

The Dutch government, however, believed that the Swedish colony was in Dutch territory. The Dutch built Fort Casimir just north of New Sweden in 1651. The Swedes captured Fort Casimir in 1654, but the Dutch took it back a year later. New Sweden was now part of New Netherland, the Dutch name for their colony.

The struggle for Delaware did not end there, however. Soon the English got involved. The English wanted to control all trade in America, but the Dutch were already starting to establish their own trading industry. In 1664 the English sent a fleet of warships to capture the Dutch forts. England's easy victory over New Netherland resulted in Delaware becoming part of the province of New York.

It was 18 years before another major change occurred in Delaware's government. William Penn was looking for a route between his colony of Pennsylvania and the Atlantic Ocean. In 1682 the Duke of York signed over to him the so-called Three Lower Counties of Delaware. Penn attempted to merge the counties with Pennsylvania, but the people of Pennsylvania and the counties objected. In 1704 he allowed Delaware to create its own legislature. Although Pennsylvania governors continued to oversee the affairs of Delaware, the people of these three counties made their own laws.

The right to make laws was one of the key issues being debated at the Continental Congress. On July 2, 1776, the delegates were arguing whether or not to declare independence from Great Britain. Differences of opinion surfaced among the delegates. Some delegates

The Zwaanendael Museum in Lewes is an exact copy of Hoorn City Hall in the Netherlands. The museum was dedicated in 1931, 300 years after the first European settlement in Delaware.

This is the site of the Battle of Cooch's Bridge. Some experts say the 13-star flag was unfurled for the first time during this battle.

wanted independence while others were undecided on the issue. Still other delegates remained loyal to the British Crown. When two of Delaware's three delegates couldn't agree, they summoned the third delegate, Caesar Rodney. He rode from Dover to Philadelphia through a severe storm to break the tie in favor of signing the Declaration of Independence. Later, all three delegates signed the document.

Delaware did not see much action during the Revolutionary War. Many Delaware soldiers took up arms, but only one battle was actually fought in the state. American troops met the British at Cooch's Bridge, near Newark, on September 3, 1777. Severely outnumbered, the Americans retreated, and the British marched on to Pennsylvania. The British occupied Wilmington nine days later. Eventually, they also captured all the forts along the Delaware River. With the British in control of the river, the capital was moved inland, from New Castle to Dover.

In 1781 the British surrendered at Yorktown, Virginia, and the war ended. Two years later, the United States was an independent nation. Delaware was very active in the organization of the new country. On December 7, 1787, Delaware became the first state to ratify the Constitution. In 1792 the state established its own state government, effectively separating itself from Pennsylvania.

Because of its central location among the Middle Atlantic states and its access to water routes, Delaware was able to build a strong economy. Wilmington had been a shipbuilding center even before the Revolutionary War. The Christina and Delaware rivers, as well as nearby Brandywine Creek, also provided excellent water power for mills. In 1785 Oliver Evans of Newport built an automatic flour-milling machine. This machine revolutionized the industry and made Delaware a major grain-milling state.

During the 1800s, industry in Delaware expanded beyond grain milling. In 1802 French immigrant Éleuthère Irénée du Pont de Nemours built a gunpowder mill on the banks of Brandywine Creek. This mill was the start of what would later become one of the biggest chemical companies in the world. Delaware was now developing chemical and textile manufacturing industries.

Delaware's industries benefited from an improved transportation system. For example, toll roads were

These men are actors at the Civil War Museum in Fort Delaware Park. During the war, the fort was a federal prison.

designed and built. The Philadelphia, Wilmington, and Baltimore Railroad was also built. In 1829 the Chesapeake and Delaware Canal, linking the two bays, was completed. An agricultural boom came to the rural portion of the state as railroad lines extended south. Slavery, which had once been useful to Delaware's agricultural economy, began to fade out—but not entirely.

When the Civil War broke out, slavery was still allowed in Delaware. In 1860 there were fewer than two thousand slaves and about twenty thousand free African Americans in Delaware. This state had much more in common with its northern neighbors—historically and economically—than with the southern states. Its citizens were divided over the slavery issue during the Civil War. The majority supported the Union, so Delaware did not secede. Many Delaware citizens, however, remained sympathetic to the South.

Fort Delaware is located on Pea Patch Island in the Delaware River. It became a prison for captured Confederate soldiers. About thirty thousand prisoners were held there from 1861 to 1865.

After the Civil War ended, laws were passed to deny African Americans their civil rights. A new law passed in 1873 made people pay a poll tax in order to vote. This excluded most African Americans, who were too poor to pay the tax. The poll tax was replaced by a literacy test in 1897. This test discriminated against people who had little education and could not read. Most African Americans had little or no opportunity to go to school. Once again, they were excluded from voting.

Economic growth in Delaware after the Civil War was centered in the Wilmington area. Corporate tax laws instituted in 1899 encouraged businesses to relocate in Wilmington. By 1920 the city contained half of Delaware's population. Pierre du Pont donated several million dollars to the state to establish a public education system for the growing population.

The industrial boom stopped in Delaware and the rest of the nation in the 1930s. The Great Depression forced millions of workers out of their jobs. Delaware citizens voted Democratic in 1932 for the first time

The Delaware Memorial Bridge connects New Castle, Delaware, to New Jersey.

since the turn of the century. Franklin D. Roosevelt became President based on his promise to pull the country out of the Depression.

As the nation entered World War II, Delaware's mills and factories produced materials for the United States military. Once again, Wilmington was the center of industrial growth and wealth. The population of the state boomed as more and more immigrants came looking for work.

In 1951 the Delaware Memorial Bridge was opened to connect Delaware's roads with New Jersey's. The bridge allowed still more factories and more people to move to Delaware.

In the 1960s, legislative districts that had long benefited the southern part of the state were redrawn. Although the majority of the people lived in the cities and suburbs, the rural areas had a stronger voice in elections. In 1968 riots by unemployed African Americans broke out in Wilmington. The violence was controlled when the National Guard was called in.

Delaware's state economy began to slow down in the 1970s. But new tax laws and other incentives changed that trend. Economic growth was further fueled in the 1980s when the state legislature passed banking laws favorable to businesses. But the state has paid a price for its economic growth in the 1990s. Urban sprawl has begun to take its toll on the environment in the form of pollution. This issue has already found its way into the state courts and the legislature, however. The debate will surely continue into the twenty-first century.

The Delaware Memorial Bridge was constructed between 1948 and 1951.

Penman of the Revolution

Have you ever heard the old saying "The pen is mightier than the sword"? It means that the written word can be more powerful than violence. That was certainly true for John Dickinson. His writings helped bring about the Revolutionary War!

When he was a young man, Dickinson studied law in London, England. He later returned to his home in the American colonies, where he practiced law before going into politics. Over the years, Dickinson was governor of both Delaware and Pennsylvania.

John Dickinson did not like the heavy taxes the American colonies were forced to pay to the British. In 1767 he began writing a series of articles against the British. The articles called on the American colonists to stop paying British taxes. Many colonists agreed with Dickinson's views, and their anger against the British grew. For two years Dickinson's articles were printed in American newspapers. Then the whole series was published in a booklet. It was titled *Letters from a Farmer in Pennsylvania to the Inhabitants of the British Colonies.* The book made John Dickinson famous. It also won him the nickname "Penman of the Revolution."

Dickinson was not in favor of the war. Although he felt the taxes were unfair, he did not want to cut all ties to the British. So when Dickinson was asked to sign the Declaration of

John Dickinson was a patriotic leader at the time of the Revolutionary War.

18

John Dickinson inherited his father's Dover plantation in 1760.

Independence in 1776, he refused. He still hoped the British and the colonists could work things out. Many colonists were surprised and angry at Dickinson's refusal. Some called him a traitor. But Dickinson proved himself a patriot. He briefly fought against the British in the Revolutionary War. After the war was over, Dickinson was one of the people who helped frame the Constitution.

John Dickinson didn't care about popular views. He knew how to think for himself. At that time, many landowners owned slaves to work the land. When Dickinson's father died, he left his two sons all his land, including sixty slaves. But John Dickinson held a different opinion concerning freedom and human rights. In 1785 he freed all his slaves.

John Dickinson is a good example of the spirit of Delaware. Free-thinking and fair-minded, the "Penman of the Revolution" ranks among the heroes of United States history.

The Tiny Giant

The little state along the Delaware River is, in its own way, an industrial giant. Its location has played a part in its growth. Four of the twenty largest cities in the nation—New York City, Philadelphia, Baltimore, and Washington, D.C.—are within a three-hour drive from Delaware. That means some people can work in Philadelphia, for example, and bring their paycheck home to Delaware. The state's economic success, however, can be attributed to two main reasons: the state's corporation laws and the Du Pont Company.

Delaware has gone out of its way to attract business and industry. For example, the Delaware legislature has reduced state corporate taxes and passed laws that make it easier for corporations to remain profitable. The result is that more than twenty-thousand corporations have offices in Delaware. In fact, more than half of the richest companies in the United States have offices in this small eastern state.

Du Pont is among the most valuable corporations in the country. The company began as a gunpowder

Wilmington, Delaware's oldest city, became a grain port in the 1730s. Today, the port is used for shipping manufactured goods as well as grains.

Wilmington is the largest community in Delaware. By 1920 half the state's population lived in Wilmington.

mill on the Brandywine Creek. Now it is one of the world's largest chemical corporations, with manufacturing plants throughout the nation and the world. The Du Pont Company plays a large role in the ongoing economic development of Delaware.

The production of manufactured goods has been steadily dropping in most eastern states. The Du Pont Company, however, has maintained its importance to manufacturing in Delaware. About 28 percent of Delaware's gross state product comes from manufacturing. Nearly one-fourth of that 28 percent comes from Du Pont's chemical manufacturing. Among the major chemical products produced in the state are nylon, dyes, and petrochemicals.

Chemical research is also very important in Delaware. Du Pont's research center near Wilmington is one of the largest chemical and medical research centers in the world. Other Wilmington chemical companies also help support chemical research. These include Hercules, Inc., and ICI Americas, Inc.

Nearly half of Delaware is farmland. About 90 percent of the state's tilled farmland is used for soybeans and corn. You might say that's not chicken feed. But it is! These crops are grown to feed the state's broiler-chicken industry. Broiler chickens are chickens that are from 5 to 12 weeks old. Delaware's ideal climate helps farmers produce three times the amount of soybeans and corn per acre that are grown in other states.

According to state historians, the modern poultry industry began in Delaware about 75 years ago. Until that time, chickens were raised mostly for the fresh eggs they produced. A woman named Cecile Steele realized she could raise chickens to sell for eating. Today, Delaware's broiler-chicken industry ranks among the largest in the nation.

Both agriculture and manufacturing are gradually becoming less important to Delaware's economy. More and more of Delaware's citizens work in jobs that do

Corn is Delaware's second most important crop.

Delaware's most profitable farm crop is broiler chickens.

23

Medical researchers at Du Pont have developed several kinds of drugs and health care products.

This technician is checking fiber structure by computerized image analysis.

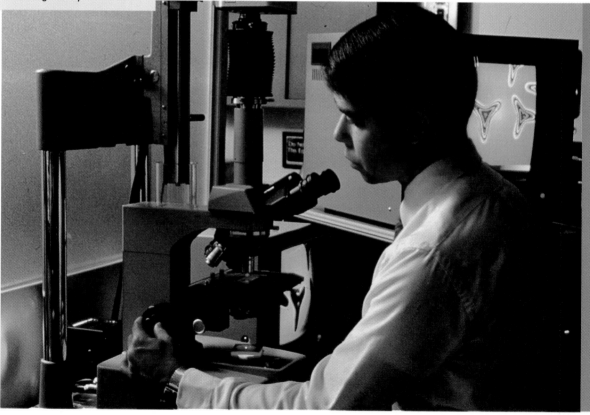

It takes about two days to make a new car from start to finish on an assembly line such as this one in Delaware. By the time the car is finished, 1,800 different operations have been performed on it.

not yield a product you can see and touch. In fact, taken as a whole, Delaware's service industries account for about two thirds of its gross state product. These industries include banking, real estate, and insurance. Most of these industries are centered in the greater Wilmington metropolitan area.

Other Delaware industries include packaging plants, textile mills, and a number of food-processing plants. Delaware also has large automobile assembly plants in Newark and Newport. Many of the people in Delaware work in management positions in companies such as Kellogg and Motorola. As a result, the average income in Delaware is about six percent higher than the national average. In fact, Delaware ranks ninth in the nation in per capita personal income.

The Bombay Hook National Wildlife Refuge sponsors many educational programs for both children and adults.

With all that industry in such a small state, it's amazing that there is any room to spare. But each year, tourists visit Delaware precisely because of its open space. It has twelve state parks, four state forests, and two national wildlife refuges that cover over 15,000 acres along the Delaware Bay.

Shore resorts also boost the tourist economy. Rehoboth Beach is the largest of Delaware's three seashore areas. The word *Rehoboth* is a biblical term

The beauty of the Delaware countryside is a crucial part of its tourist industry.

Rehoboth Beach in southern Delaware is known as the Nation's Summer Capital because so many visitors come from Washington, D.C.

meaning "wide spaces." Nothing could be truer. Residents in Rehoboth say that their town's population multiplies by ten in the summer months.

Maybe Delaware isn't so tiny after all. It certainly has had enough room to draw the kind of businesses that have kept the state's economy healthy.

This is the Ruddertown Lighthouse at Dewey Beach. The Rehoboth Beach/Dewey Beach area has been popular since the 1870s, when it was used for Methodist church meetings.

A Business Built on Explosives

The du Pont family and their company, E. I. du Pont de Nemours and Company, have been an important contributor to Delaware for almost two hundred years. Today, the family fortune is estimated at more than $8.6 billion. But this family's success hasn't come easily—each generation has had to work hard and pull its own weight.

In 1800 Pierre Samuel du Pont de Nemours moved his family from France to Delaware. Pierre's younger son Éleuthère Irénée wanted to start a business in this new country. He got an idea during a hunting expedition in the Brandywine Valley one day. After missing many shots because of the poor quality of American gunpowder, he decided to start a gunpowder business. Du Pont knew something about the properties of gunpowder. He had studied in France with the famous chemist Antoine Lavoisier. He was convinced he could make a much better gunpowder at a cheaper price than other American companies. In 1802 he built his gunpowder company on the banks of the Brandywine Creek.

By the time Éleuthère Irénée died in 1834, his mills were producing over one million pounds of gunpowder a year. His gunpowder was used to help defeat the British in the War of 1812. Later, during the Civil War, it was Du Pont gunpowder that packed the muskets of the Union soldiers.

But by this time the company had already expanded on its product.

Éleuthère Irénée du Pont never saw the financial success his company would become. When he died, the company was $125,000 in debt. The Du Pont Company did not begin to prosper until the early 1900s.

The original du Pont house and gardens is now the Hagley Museum and Library. It is located in Wilmington, near the first Du Pont powder mill.

The United States was branching out. Canals and railroads needed soda powder to blast their way into new frontiers. So the mills expanded to make soda powder for blasting. Gold and silver mines needed plenty of explosives, too. The company's profits skyrocketed.

The du Ponts stuck to making explosives for almost a hundred years. At the turn of the century, Du Pont started to buy out its competitors. By 1905 the company was producing about 75 percent of all the explosive powder in the United States. But the government decided that it was dangerous to let one business have complete control over one type of product. So in 1912 the government forced the du Ponts to sell some of their powder plants.

That didn't bother the du Ponts, however. They simply looked for new products to produce. They focused the company's research on chemicals. Du Pont became one of the largest chemical companies in the world.

Beginning in 1915, Du Pont developed and produced hundreds of new items, such as fertilizers, dyes, cloth, rubber, and plastics. Perhaps you've heard of Lucite, Teflon, Orlon, Lycra, or Dacron. All of these useful materials were created by Du Pont. Their researchers also invented nylon and the refrigerant Freon.

Many members of the du Pont family shared their profits with the community and the state. Pierre Samuel du Pont was the most generous of all. In 1929 he donated one million dollars to various Delaware organizations. It was estimated that over his lifetime he donated over one billion dollars to various charities. That's a lot of money now, but a billion dollars was worth considerably more in 1929 than it is today! He also helped to build public schools and roads that are still used today.

The du Ponts have helped Delaware in other ways, also. Some family members have donated their estates to have them turned into museums. Thousands of tourists a year come to see the Hagley Museum and Library, the Nemours Mansion, and the Winterthur Museum.

Pierre "Pete" du Pont IV, in his two terms as governor in the 1970s and 1980s, helped the state to pull out of its worst economic crisis ever. Pete explained how he did it with the help of the Delaware legislature. "We came to recognize . . . that we were all in this together. And instead of one of us putting water into the boat, we decided to take our buckets and everybody bail water out."

So thanks to the family spirit of Pete du Pont, the political leaders of Delaware decided to forget about who was going to get credit for solving the problems and who was going to get

An exterior view of the main building at the Winterthur Museum.

Pete du Pont served two terms as governor of Delaware in the 1970s and 1980s.

blamed. Business leaders noticed. As Mr. du Pont said, "They were astonished that here in one room were all the decision makers, including the mayor and the governor, who would directly impact the things that were going to happen to their business in Delaware." Business leaders were impressed enough to take a chance on Delaware, and the state's economy was saved.

Delawareans may sometimes wonder where they would be today if the du Ponts had not settled in their state. The name du Pont has meant many things to Delaware—benefactor, employer, and political leader.

Du Pont's experimental complex near Brandywine Creek is just one of its many research facilities.

31

City Homesteaders

In the early 1970s, the city of Wilmington had about 1,500 vacant houses that were boarded up. The city was in an economic slump, and not many people were buying houses. Not only were these abandoned houses an eyesore in the neighborhoods, they were also dangerous. Kids wanted to play inside them, and somebody was going to get hurt. The city came up with a very creative way to turn these houses into homes. Wilmington became the first city in the nation to start a homesteading program. The city sold the vacant houses for low prices to people who agreed to fix them up.

Actually, the agreements that Wilmington offered to participants in the homesteading program had been done on a larger scale before. The plan was similar to the one the United States government offered to settlers of the American West and Alaska. Beginning in the 1860s, the federal government either gave large tracts of land away or sold them at very low prices. In exchange the settlers promised a five-year commitment to improve the land. These deals helped early settlers to own homesteads, or small farms, of their own.

Wilmington's city homesteaders didn't start farms. But in a time when housing was difficult to afford, they were proud to have houses of their own. And what did Wilmington get in return? Neighborhoods that were on the verge of becoming slums soon

Dan and Bonnie Frawley prepare to reno-vate their new homestead.

changed into thriving communities. Many cities have spent millions of dollars trying to do what Wilmington did for almost no cost.

Terry and Sally O'Byrne bought a house early in the program. Terry recalls, "When we saw this home-steading program, we put in for a house. But I was thinking there's some catch here. People don't give away houses. But they did." The O'Byrnes bought their house for a dollar. They spent a lot of money fixing it up, but it was worth it. In 1977 they sold their house at a standard rate and were then able to buy a larger house

for their growing family. The home-steading program was just the start they needed.

By 1989 Wilmington had gotten back on its feet and decided to end the program. But people like the O'Byrnes are glad to have been a part of it. And the city of Wilmington is proud to have neighborhoods of well-built houses and dedicated homeown-ers instead of slums.

Dan and Bonnie Frawley pose outside their restored homestead.

Thomas Maloney, mayor of Wilmington, testified about his city before the United States House Subcommittee on Government Operations in June 1975.

A Cache of Delaware Traditions

In the Brandywine Valley, near Wilmington, stands the Winterthur Museum. Inside it are displays of two hundred rooms from the past. Each room is decorated with chairs, tables, china, silver—all made by craftspeople between 1640 and 1860.

Folklife is a word that refers to shared common tradition and heritage. In fact, the people of Delaware value their traditions so much that they have set up the Delaware Folklife Program. Supporters of this program gather, interpret, and record many kinds of Delaware folklife, past and present. They then work to share this information with the residents of Delaware and the rest of the nation.

Delaware's taste for tradition extends beyond the Folklife Program, however. For instance, Wilmington hosts the Delaware Symphony Orchestra and the OperaDelaware in its Grand Opera House. Built in 1871, the design of the Grand is based on the Second Empire period of French architecture. This traditional style has been maintained inside as well as outside.

Brandywine Creek State Park is home to Delaware's first two nature preserves, the Tulip Tree Woods and the Freshwater Marsh.

The Grand Opera House in Wilmington dates back to the mid-nineteenth century. It is the home of the Delaware Symphony Orchestra and the OperaDelaware.

This house in Milton is one of many on the National Register of Historic Places.

The Opera House is filled with plush velvet, polished brass, winding staircases, and ceilings with frescoes. Just north of Wilmington is the village of Arden. This village was founded by artists and craftspeople in 1900. Its theatrical traditions include annual productions of Gilbert and Sullivan operettas.

Another example of preserving tradition is in the town of Milton. The town was named for the poet John Milton. Milton has many fine examples of eighteenth- and nineteenth-century American architecture. In fact, 198 homes in Milton are on the National Register of Historic Places. Also on the register are the Historic Houses of Odessa, which are owned and operated by the Winterthur Museum. The Corbit-Sharp House in

The Corbit-Sharp House in Odessa is furnished to look the way it would have in the late eighteenth century. The house was built by William Corbit in 1774. In 1938 Rodney Sharp restored it and donated the house to the Winterthur Museum.

The Winterthur Museum has many full-size period rooms, or rooms decorated just as they would have been in different time periods.

Alfred I. du Pont modeled Nemours Mansion and Gardens after the style of the French king Louis XVI.

Odessa contains furnishings that illustrate life from 1774 to 1818. Other houses also contain traditional furniture. At some houses, visitors can see demonstrations of traditional chores, such as hearth cooking. Visitors can also participate in craft workshops.

Delaware's oldest traditions are also preserved. The Nanticokes of Sussex County were Delaware's first residents. The Nanticoke Pow Wow is an event that is held every September. The Nanticokes invite their remaining members and the public for two days of ceremonial dancing, storytelling, and Native American crafts and food.

Located so close to New York, Philadelphia, and Washington, D.C., the state of Delaware could easily be overshadowed. But Delaware's rich heritage, natural beauty, and proud residents make this state difficult to ignore.

Weaving a Piece of History

Joe Hughes, a Delaware farmer and basket maker, knows Delaware folklife firsthand. His family has been farming in Kent County for eight generations. It's the importance of folklife that convinced him to carry on that tradition.

When Joe was drafted into the army, he was young and eager to get out of Delaware and see the world. Joe remembers when his father came to the bus station to see him off. "I said to him, 'Well, you'll never see me back on that mudhole again.' But I wasn't gone too long before I wanted to come back. I've been here ever since."

Joe Hughes's basket weaving carries on a form of folk art that was once crucial to Delaware residents living off the land. Many of the weaving patterns he uses have been passed down over generations of basket makers since colonial times. As Joe says, "When I sit here and make baskets, I feel it's very much a timeless thing. I could be here a hundred years ago doing this. It's a complete escape from the modern world and all its associated technology. I'm in touch with the past and with something that's now."

Today, Joe shares this folk history with the young people of Delaware. He participates in Traditional Artists in Residence, a community resource started by the Delaware Folklife Program. Schools and community centers can apply to invite Joe or other folk artists to stay in their community for three days to two weeks. Program participants make items such as duck

Joe Hughes weaves his baskets from white oaks. He cuts, splits, shapes, and weaves the oaks by hand.

decoys, musical instruments, and fishing nets. All of these are made with skills that have been carried down over the generations by Delaware residents. During their stay, the artists teach students not only the craft itself but also the state history and culture that surround the craft. The program has been a huge success so far. It has led these craftspeople to organize a yearly folk festival. This way the entire community, not just students, can learn from their skills.

"The greatest satisfaction in basketry," says Joe, "is the fact that you can go into the woods, . . . find the proper tree, cut that tree down, tear it apart pretty much with your bare hands, and make something useful out of it." Joe Hughes and the Delaware

Joe Hughes's farm is located in Kent County, west of Fulton. Hughes learned from his father how to use natural resources carefully.

Folklife Program hope to pass this feeling of satisfaction on to generations to come. With the help of Delaware folk artists, students and other community members learn much more than how to make a basket. They learn how to reconstruct a part of history. It's the best—and most lasting—type of history lesson anyone can learn.

The Port Penn Wetland Folk Festival celebrates traditions that are a part of wetlands life in Delaware, such as trapping, fishing, and hunting.

A Big Future for a Small State

"I am convinced that Delaware has the potential to become a model state. The state that started a nation can also lead a nation." Russell Peterson, Delaware governor from 1969 to 1973, spoke those optimistic words while the state was in one of the worst financial situations in the country. Today, Delaware has completely turned itself around. The unemployment rate is well below the national average, and incomes are above average.

The state's commitment to research and development promises to keep the state's economy moving forward. Du Pont and Du Pont Merck medical researchers have five major laboratories in Delaware, which employ over half of Du Pont's worldwide research staff. Hercules, ICI Americas, and other companies also help to keep Delaware at the forefront of chemical and medical research.

But all this growth presents special problems for a state this size. Is there room for all these companies in a state smaller than some counties in other states? So

Wilmington is known as the "Chemical Capital of the World." Chemical companies employ about one third of Wilmington's workforce.

far, the answer seems to be yes. But it is going to take wisdom on the part of the people of Delaware to make things work.

Some of that wisdom is already being put to use. Delaware was one of the first states to pass strict pollution laws. In 1971 it passed the Coastal Zone Act to prevent heavy industrial development along the coast. Today the state works hard to make sure this act's strict rules are followed. Delaware still has one of the most natural coastal areas of any of the Middle Atlantic states. The challenge is to keep it that way.

Delaware consistently comes out at the top of lists for high quality of life and a low cost of living. But this state doesn't need lists and rankings to prove its advantages. They're right there for all to see. Clean air, unspoiled coasts and marshes, and respect for the past are what make the people of Delaware proud. These elements, combined with one of the healthiest economies in the nation, have made the future bright for this gem of a state.

Delaware's industrial growth all takes place within the context of strict pollution laws. These houses in the Brandywine Valley are only a short distance from one of Wilmington's industrial complexes.

1609 Henry Hudson goes through Delaware Bay to explore the Delaware River.

1610 Samuel Argall names the bay after Virginia governor Lord De La Warr.

1631 The first European settlement in Delaware is established by the Dutch at Zwaanendael, now Lewes.

1632 The settlement is destroyed by coastal Native Americans.

1638 Swedish colonists build Fort Christina, now Wilmington. It is the first permanent settlement in Delaware.

1651 Dutch settlers build Fort Casimir just above New Sweden.

1655 The Dutch governor of New Amsterdam sends forces to conquer New Sweden and incorporate it into the New Netherland colony.

1664 To eliminate Dutch trading competition in the American colonies, the English attack the Dutch colonies. Delaware becomes part of the province of New York.

1682 The Duke of York gives the Delaware counties to William Penn, founder of Pennsylvania.

1704 Penn permits the people of Delaware to form their own legislature. They share Pennsylvania's governor but make their own laws.

1739 The Borough of Wilmington is given a royal charter.

1776 Delaware delegates sign the Declaration of Independence. Delaware breaks from Pennsylvania and writes its own constitution.

1777 The British Army invades Delaware. After the British seize Wilmington and the Delaware River, the state capital is moved from New Castle to Dover.

1785 Oliver Evans of Newport builds an automatic flour mill.

1787 Delaware is the first state to ratify the United States Constitution.

1792 The second state constitution is ratified.

1802 The Du Pont industrial empire is founded when E. I. du Pont opens a gunpowder mill on Brandywine Creek.

1813 The fishing village of Lewes holds out against British bombardment in the War of 1812.

1831 The third state constitution is adopted.

1861 Although a slave state, Delaware refuses to secede from the Union.

1897 The fourth, and present, state constitution is adopted.

1917 A state highway department is instituted.

1939 Nylon is manufactured at the Du Pont plant in Seaford.

1951 The Delaware Memorial Bridge links Delaware with New Jersey.

1971 The Delaware Coastal Zone Act forbids construction of industrial plants in the coastal areas of Delaware.

1981 The Delaware Development Office is established to help the state's businesses and workers.

1993 The number of jobs in Delaware climbs to 3,500 over the previous year. Unemployment remains lower than the national average.

The flag has a background of colonial blue surrounding a diamond of buff color in which the coat of arms of the state is placed. The symbols on the coat of arms indicate agriculture and the sea, flanked on either side by a farmer and a soldier. Below the diamond are the words "December 7, 1787." This is the day on which Delaware became the first state in the Union.

DECEMBER 7, 1787

Delaware Almanac

Nickname. The First State

Capital. Dover

State Bird. Blue hen chicken

State Flower. Peach blossom

State Tree. American holly

State Motto. Liberty and Independence

State Song. "Our Delaware"

State Abbreviations. Del. (traditional); DE (postal)

Statehood. December 7, 1787, the first state

Government. Congress: U.S. senators, 2; U.S. representatives, 1. State Legislature: senators, 21; representatives, 41. Counties: 3

Area. 2,044 sq mi (5,294 sq km), 49th in size among the states

Greatest Distances. north/south, 96 mi (155 km); east/west, 39 mi (63 km). Coastline: 28 mi (45 km)

Elevation. Highest: 442 ft (135 m). Lowest: sea level, along the coastline

Population. 1990 Census: 668,696 (12.5% increase over 1980), 46th among the states. Density: 330 persons per sq mi (127 persons per sq km). Distribution: 73% urban, 27% rural. 1980 Census: 594,338

Economy. Agriculture: broilers (young chickens), soybeans, corn, potatoes. Fishing: crabs, clams. Manufacturing: chemicals, food products, paper and plastic products, automobiles. Mining: magnesium, sand, gravel

State Seal

State Flower: Peach blossom

State Bird: Blue hen chicken

Annual Events

★ Delaware Gem and Mineral Show in Claymont (March)

★ Easter Promenade at Rehoboth Beach (Easter Sunday)

★ Great Delaware Kite Festival in Lewes (April)

★ Delmarva Hot Air Balloon Festival in Milton (May)

★ Dover Air Force Base Airshow (May)

★ Old Dover Days (May)

★ Delaware Stock Car Races in Dover (September)

★ Nanticoke Indian Pow Wow in Millsboro (September)

★ Sea Witch Halloween Festival in Rehoboth Beach (October)

★ Bombay Hook Field Day in Smyrna (November)

★ Christmas Candlelight Tours at Hagley Museum, near Wilmington (December)

Places to Visit

★ Amstel House Museum in New Castle

★ Bombay Hook National Wildlife Refuge in Smyrna

★ Cooch's Bridge in Newark

★ Dover Air Force Base

★ Hagley Museum Historic Site, near Wilmington

★ John Dickinson Plantation in Dover

★ Nemours Mansion and Gardens in Wilmington

★ Old State House in Dover

★ Old Swedes Church and Hendrickson House Museum in Wilmington

★ Shore areas, such as Rehoboth Beach, Bethany Beach, and Fenwick Island

★ Winterthur Museum, Garden, and Library in Winterthur

★ Zwaanendael Museum in Lewes